You are approached by two look-alike snakes.
You know that one of them is poisonous,
but you don't know which one. You wisely decide
to leave. But which one is the poisonous one?
(See page 22)

You are at the seashore, picking up
some seashells. You find the big, strange shell
of a horseshoe crab, which isn't a crab at all.
But if it isn't a crab, what is it?
(See page 31)

You are on vacation in Florida.
A crocodile and an alligator stroll by.
Do you know which is which?
(See pages 26-27)

to Holly and Will

JOE KAUFMAN'S

Slimy, Creepy, Crawly Creatures

Written and Illustrated by JOE KAUFMAN

DR. JOHN A. VAN COUVERING, Consultant
American Museum of Natural History

A GOLDEN BOOK • NEW YORK
Western Publishing Company, Inc. Racine, Wisconsin 53404

In Devonshire, England, people who believed in witches also believed that TOADS had anti-witch powers.

Mesopotamian soldiers watched ANTS. If the ants fought, the enemy was approaching.

CONTENTS

A NOTE TO PARENTS: This book, designed as a companion to Mr. Kaufman's earlier book about mammals and birds, is about fish, amphibians, reptiles, mollusks, insects, and arachnids. In entertaining, accurate text and detailed pictures, the author introduces readers to the biggest fish in the world, reveals the difference between an alligator and a crocodile, shows how a snake can swallow an egg wider than itself, tells why bees "dance," how a spider spins its web, and much, much more. The book is intended for children 6 to 12 years old, but will appeal to any young reader with a bent for natural science—or a love of slimy, creepy, crawly creatures.

There's a belief in the Ozark Mountains that if a BEE buzzes around your head, you'll receive a letter with money in it.

In Malaya, people believed that if a LIZARD entered a house, troubles would also enter. To avoid the troubles they would sprinkle the lizard with ashes.

An old English superstition: a black SNAIL crossing anyone's path is a sure sign of rain.

In parts of western Europe some people believe that if you eat a raw HERRING, you will have a vision of your future spouse.

SUPERSTITIONS

SUPERSTITIONS about animals are still believed in some parts of the world. A superstition is something people believe without having a good reason. Some familiar ones are that the number 13 is unlucky and that walking under a ladder brings bad luck, or that finding a 4-leaf clover or a horseshoe brings good luck. We don't know how old these superstitions are, but they've been around for a long time.

There are many superstitions about animals and their magic powers. Long ago, some people thought that a cure for whooping cough was to tie a beetle to a thread and hang it around a sick child's neck. Eating snake eggs was believed to be a remedy for stuttering, and wearing a rattlesnake's rattle in your hatband was supposed to prevent rheumatism. In many places, frogs and toads were considered good luck omens. People thought that if you made a wish when you saw the first frog in spring, your wish would come true. A toad crossing the path of a bridal party on its way to church brought prosperity and happiness. A praying mantis was another good omen. If one happened to land on your head, you could expect to receive a very special honor.

Another old belief was that a foggy day would turn bright if you took a turtle out of water and placed it on the ground. A bumblebee in the house meant you would have a visitor. To have good luck, all you had to do was to throw a hairy caterpillar over your left shoulder or carry a rabbit's foot with you. As long as superstitions are handed down, somebody somewhere will believe them.

A sailor's superstition: a SHARK following a ship brings bad luck, especially if sick people are aboard.

Another Ozark superstition: if two SNAKES come into a house, there will soon be a wedding.

EXTINCT FISH, amphibians, reptiles, insects, and other animals died out when their surroundings and food supplies changed and they could not adapt to the changes. Those animals that could adapt to the new situation survived. And new species evolved that thrived on the new environment. But exactly what caused the disappearance of each type of animal is not yet known. All the dinosaurs became extinct about 70 million years ago—scientists aren't yet sure why.

Meganeurons, the largest insects ever to exist, were the giants of the early insect world.

Dimetrodons were sharp-toothed, meat-eating reptiles that lived about 250 million years ago.

Bradysaurs were plant-eaters. They used their big grinding teeth to chew tough plants.

Tanystrophs, with very long necks that moved quickly, could probably catch insects and fish.

Cynognaths, mammal-like reptiles, had powerful jaws and ate both meat and plants.

Euparkerias walked slowly on all fours, but in a fast chase used only their strong hind legs.

Plesiosaurs, whose flexible necks contained up to 76 bones, swam as gracefully as today's seals.

Arthropleurs, with many-jointed bodies, squirmed through the swamps, looking for leafy food.

Labyrinthodonts sometimes lived on land and sometimes in water.

Tylosaurs were giant fish-eaters. They had sharp teeth that could crush the shells of big shellfish.

Dinichthys were probably slow swimmers. They had powerful jaws that snapped shut like a trap.

Nautiloids came in a variety of sizes. Some were straight, and some were curled up. Today's nautilus is the descendant of a 500-million-year-old family.

DIMETRODONS were large reptiles with high crests on their backs that helped regulate their temperatures.

CYNOGNATHS were the size of very large dogs. Two of their teeth were long, sharp tusks.

PLESIOSAURS were long-necked reptiles that lived in the sea. They swam by using their legs as paddles.

TYLOSAURS, enormous swimming lizards with sharp teeth, were sometimes as long as 48 feet.

In 1938, fishermen caught a COELACANTH, a fish scientists believed had been extinct for 7 million years.

8

MEGANEURONS were huge dragonflies with 30-inch wingspreads.

BRADYSAURS were husky, one-ton, 9-foot-long members of the cotylosaur family, the first reptiles.

TANYSTROPHS were snake-like reptiles that sometimes reached 20 feet in length.

EUPARKERIAS were land reptiles. Their long hind legs made them swift hunters of smaller animals.

ARTHROPLEURS looked like our centipedes, but were gigantic. Some were as long as 6 feet.

LABYRINTHODONTS were large amphibians, some as big as crocodiles.

DINICHTHYS were huge fish with heavily armored heads. Some were 25 feet long.

Giant NAUTILOIDS, 15 feet long, were early ancestors of our squids and octopuses.

DOGFISH are small sharks with eel-like bodies.

GIANT SEA BASS may grow to weigh as much as 600 lbs. and reach 7 ft. in length.

SHARKS have skeletons made of cartilage, not bone. They have no scales.

BLUEFISH swim in huge groups and attack smaller fish.

GROUPERS are a part of the large sea bass family.

HADDOCK are many people's favorite food fish from the Atlantic.

HAKE are part of the large cod family.

MULLETS, good food fish, are often caught in nets and smoked.

SALTWATER FISH spend all their time in salt water, and many are so accustomed to it that if they were put into fresh water they would die. They must have just the right amount of salt in their bodies—less than there is in ocean water, but more than in fresh water. The extra salt is taken out of the water inside their bodies and eliminated. Fish made their appearance on earth about 500 million years ago. They were the first animals to have a backbone.

Animals with backbones are called vertebrates.

Different kinds of saltwater fish are used to different water temperatures. Since fish are cold-blooded (as are all animals except birds and mammals), their body temperature is almost the same as that of the water around them. For that reason most saltwater fish live in warmer waters. Different saltwater fish live at different levels in the water. Some live near the sunny surface, some in the darker

Deep-sea fishing as a sport is very popular. The fish are caught with only a rod and reel.

TUNA are large cousins of mackerels.

SAILFISH are some of the fastest swimmers.

RED SNAPPERS live mostly in the Gulf of Mexico.

MARLINS are a favorite catch of sport fishermen. They battle when hooked.

BARRACUDA are fierce fighters with powerful jaws.

BONEFISH are difficult for fishermen to catch.

MACKERELS have streamlined bodies.

TARPONS can make spectacular leaps out of the water.

mid-depths, while other kinds prefer the black, gloomy waters near the ocean's bottom.

Commercial fishing for saltwater fish along coastlines went on for centuries. When ways were developed to keep fish from spoiling and improved ships were built, commercial fishing spread out into deeper seas. Today fleets of trawlers from many countries cast their nets into the ocean in places where fishermen expect fish to be. These ships can

stay out a long time because they are equipped with modern freezing equipment. Unfortunately, some species have been overfished and are becoming rare.

Game fishing in ocean waters is a sport that many people enjoy. Game fish are caught with a rod and reel, but they are not the kind of fish that go limp when they are hooked and let themselves be pulled in. Instead, they put up a tough fight to get away—and often succeed.

11

CHUB, cousins of carp, are caught in European rivers and lakes.

SUNFISH are small and easy for girls and boys to catch.

YELLOW BASS are a favorite and delicious catch.

BREAM are European. They have small mouths and wide bodies.

PICKEREL are small members of the pike family.

GRAYLINGS have long, high dorsal fins.

TENCH are found in Europe and Asia. Their color changes as they age.

RAINBOW TROUT, once found only in western U.S. waters, now flourish in many other places.

SOCKEYE SALMON males turn red during the mating season.

FRESHWATER FISH usually

stay in fresh water, and many couldn't live at all in salt water. But some, such as the salmon, are born in fresh water, spend part of their life in salt water, then return to fresh water.

Most freshwater fish have the same kind of body as saltwater fish. It is streamlined and has scales and teeth. The skeleton has a skull, backbone, ribs, and rays for fins and tail. (Rays are rods that support

the fins.) The skin is covered with a slimy coating.

A fish's fins and tail are its swimming equipment. The tail moves from side to side and pushes the fish forward; the fins do the steering. Most fish have an air bladder inside to keep them afloat. They have gills to take in oxygen. People get oxygen by breathing air. A fish gets oxygen this way: first water enters its mouth and passes over the gills on each side of its head. Then the blood, circulating through the

YELLOW PERCHES are the best known of the large perch family.

CHAR are also called brook trout and live in streams and lakes of N. America and Europe

BURBOT are the only freshwater fish in the cod family.

BLUE CATFISH are the biggest of all catfish.

SUCKERS have mouths that can suck up their food.

BOWFINS have thick bodies like tubes.

AYUS are Japanese fish much like salmon.

CARP were brought from Asia to Europe and America.

gills, takes oxygen from the water. The oxygen goes in the bloodstream and travels through the body. The water leaves the body of the fish through the gill valves, and then the breathing process begins again.

Freshwater fishing has always been enjoyed by people of all ages. If you want to try fishing and can get to a stream or lake, you don't need a lot of expensive equipment. Find a store that sells fishing supplies. Buy a bamboo pole about 10 feet long—they come in 1 piece or 2 or 3 pieces that you put together. You'll need some fishing line (nylon is best), a few floats, and some hooks that are the right size for the fish's mouth. At home, tie the line to the end of the fishing pole, then cut the line to make it a foot longer than the pole. Fasten a float about 3 feet from the end of the line. Tie a hook to the end. Now you're ready to go out, put a worm on the hook, cast the line into the water, and wait patiently for the first bite.

13

FLYING FISH can leap out of the water, spread their wing-like fins, and glide for 500 to 600 feet.

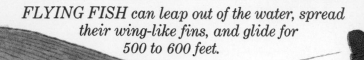

An *ELECTRIC EEL* can give off enough current to light an electric bulb.

An *ARCHERFISH* finds an insect sitting on a leaf above. The fish puts its snout out of the water, squirts water at the insect, knocks it into the water, and eats it.

When a *PUFFER* feels that it is being attacked, it puffs up like a balloon to scare the enemy away.

Although the *WHALE SHARK* is the biggest of all fish (up to 50 feet long), it is very peaceful, and harmless to people. Divers sometimes climb on its back.

Deep in the ocean in almost complete darkness live weird-looking *ANGLERFISH*. Each has a glowing light at the end of a sort of little "fishing pole" that lures other fish close enough to eat.

ceratioid angler

blackdevil angler

Johnson's angler

14

UNUSUAL FISH may be just ordinary fish to their friends and foes who live in the water, but they are full of surprises to people who first see them and learn about them. There are 23,000 kinds of fish in the oceans, lakes, rivers, and other bodies of water that cover more than 2/3 of the earth's surface. There are more fish, and more kinds of fish, than any other animal with a backbone. Some of the most unusual ones are listed below.

Flying fish, in order to take off from the water, swim at terrific speed, about 40 miles an hour. They "fly" to escape from larger fish that may want to eat them, and they sometimes land on a passing boat.

Electric eels, which are often seen lighting bulbs in aquariums, are natives of South America. They stun the fish they hunt with electric shocks.

Seahorses don't look like fish. They swim upright — fish don't do that! They hold on to seaweed with

The SEA HORSE mother puts her eggs in the father's pouch. The eggs develop and hatch inside the pouch.

After a few weeks, the father knows that the babies are ready to leave. He gently pushes out the tiny sea horses.

their tails — fish don't do that! They have no scales. Yet experts say they're fish.

Archerfish are small freshwater fish that feed on insects. They seek out their prey by swimming into muddy waters and peeking out. When they see a victim, they perform their water-squirting feat.

Whale sharks often travel in groups. They eat tiny sea plants and animals, letting the food flow into their wide mouths. Imagine seeing a group of friendly sharks, big as whales, coming toward you with their mouths open!

Puffers puff up when threatened. Some gulp air, others gulp water, still others gulp air and water. When the threat is gone they deflate by belching out the air or water until they are normal size again.

Deep-sea anglerfish are unusual not only because of their glowing lures, but also because the males are tiny. Females are over 3 feet long; males are only 3-1/3 inches long.

FISH as PETS

Fish need a 10 to 20 gallon tank with a lid to keep them from jumping out,

and a pump with a filter to keep the water clean.

filter

pump

You'll need a heater to keep the water at just the right temperature and also a thermometer for testing.

Add some medium-sized gravel for the bottom...

and some useful, attractive plants.

Now choose some aquarium fish. There are many kinds.

Comet

Wakin

Swordtail

And you'll need the right fish food.

Your aquarium is complete. Have fun taking good care of it.

How far can you jump? Some frogs can leap more than 20 times the length of their bodies.

The PIG FROG grunts like a pig.

The BULLFROG is the biggest N. American frog.

The GREEN FROG lives close to shallow water.

The LEOPARD FROG is mostly active at night.

The RED-LEGGED FROG likes damp woods.

The MARSH FROG lives mostly in Europe.

The GIANT TOAD likes heat and humidity.

FOWLER'S TOAD is also a night hunter.

The GREEN TOAD lives in dry climates.

FROGS and **TOADS** are amphibians, the kind of animal that developed after fish and before reptiles. They were the ones that first tried leaving the water and crawling around on land. And, to this day, most amphibians spend part of their life in water and part on land.

Frogs and toads look alike, and people have trouble telling one from the other. But there are differences. Frogs are smooth and moist, while toads are dry and bumpy. Frogs have long legs and can jump long distances. Toads, with shorter legs, can't jump as far. Frogs have upper teeth; toads are toothless. Toads are plumper than frogs. Frogs live in water or wet places; toads prefer moist land. And, remember, frogs and toads don't cause warts. Warts are rough bumps of skin you get from a virus.

Frogs and toads lay their thousands of eggs in water, in a sort of jelly. Even when they live on land,

Most frogs are born in water and change from egg to frog in these stages:

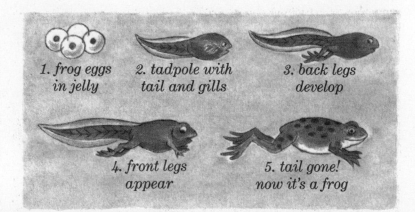

1. frog eggs in jelly
2. tadpole with tail and gills
3. back legs develop
4. front legs appear
5. tail gone! now it's a frog

Frogs grow in many ways. The Darwin frog in Chile does this: the male takes the eggs into his mouth; they develop inside until they hop out as complete little frogs.

actual size: 1 inch

16

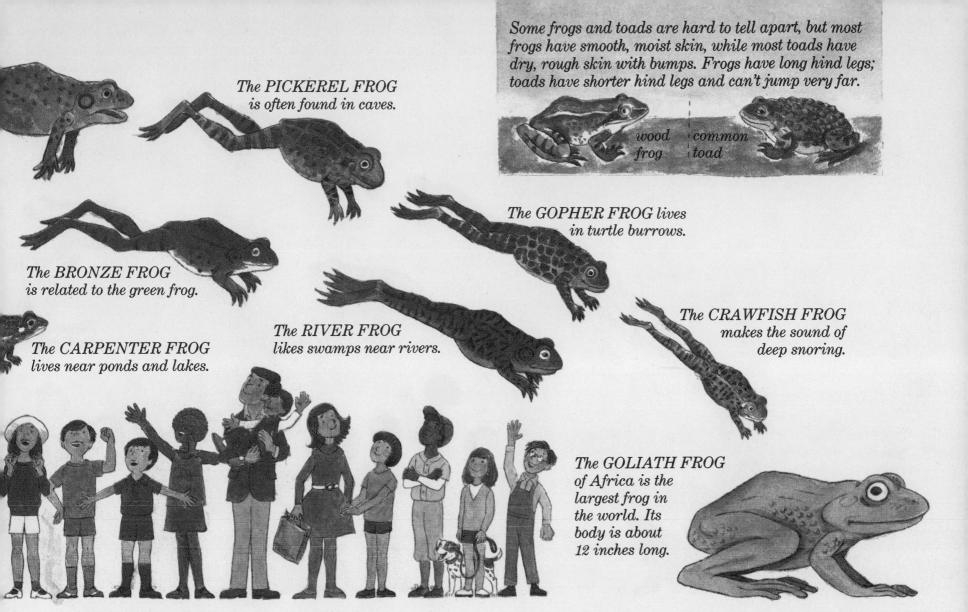

The PICKEREL FROG is often found in caves.

Some frogs and toads are hard to tell apart, but most frogs have smooth, moist skin, while most toads have dry, rough skin with bumps. Frogs have long hind legs; toads have shorter hind legs and can't jump very far.

wood frog | common toad

The GOPHER FROG lives in turtle burrows.

The BRONZE FROG is related to the green frog.

The CARPENTER FROG lives near ponds and lakes.

The RIVER FROG likes swamps near rivers.

The CRAWFISH FROG makes the sound of deep snoring.

The GOLIATH FROG of Africa is the largest frog in the world. Its body is about 12 inches long.

frogs and toads return to water to lay eggs. Soon the eggs develop into young tadpoles that look like little fish. They even breathe through gills as fish do. But when the tadpoles grow into adults, they lose their gills and tail, and develop legs. Now they're ready for life on land or in water.

Frogs and toads mostly eat insects, and catch them with their very long tongues. Their tongues can be flicked out to catch insects with lightning speed.

The smallest frog is the inch-long Darwin frog and the largest is the Goliath frog, which measures up to 16 inches long. Frogs have very bulgy eyes with an extra set of transparent eyelids that allow them to keep their eyes open under water. Behind their eyes are two flat discs which are their eardrums; they have no outer ears. A frog sheds its skin quite often. Using its forelegs, the frog just pulls off its old skin like a sweater, then swallows it.

Just an ordinary day in the life of a frog:

tries to keep well hidden from its enemies

flips out its long tongue to catch a meal on land

leaps out of the water for another meal

sings a song with closed mouth and puffed throat

jug-o-rum

17

LAND SALAMANDERS, also called terrestrial salamanders, spend most of their time on land.

LONG-TAILED SALAMANDERS are about the thinnest salamanders for their length (5 inches).

WESTERN NEWTS and their eastern cousins make excellent salamander pets.

SPOTTED SALAMANDERS live in the area from Nova Scotia to Texas.

RED SALAMANDERS live in northeast U.S. Their bright red darkens as they get old.

BANDED SALAMANDERS are found in many parts of Europe. Some have 2 long back stripes.

TIGER SALAMANDERS live in parts of Canada, United States, and Mexico. They have bright, bold patterns.

WATER SALAMANDERS, also called marine salamanders, spend most of their time in the water.

CONGO "EELS" are salamanders that look enough like eels to fool people. You must look carefully for their miniature legs.

4 tiny legs

MUD PUPPIES are salamanders that have bright red gills. They keep these gills all through life.

HELLBENDERS, salamanders that are big and flat, are covered with loose skin through which they get oxygen.

GREAT SIRENS, the kind of salamanders that have only front legs, live in water in southern U.S.

2 tiny legs

DUSKY SALAMANDERS live in or near streams. Their dark skins blend with moss and rocks.

PACIFIC GIANT SALAMANDERS, 1 ft. long, the biggest U.S. land species, can climb 8 ft. trees.

SALAMANDERS, like frogs and toads, are amphibians. Although salamanders look like lizards, they are not. Lizards are reptiles, as are snakes, crocodiles, and turtles.

There are 450 different kinds of salamanders. Some are brightly colored, while others have darker, grayer skin. Most salamanders are small, but some grow to be up to 5 feet long.

Salamanders have smooth, moist skin, which they shed often as they grow. Their legs are short, with 4 toes on each front foot and 5 toes on each back foot. Both their upper and lower jaws have teeth. If a salamander loses a leg or a tail, a new one will soon grow to replace it.

Some salamanders live in streams or ponds and eat by sucking tiny water animals into their mouths. Others live on land in dark, moist places, hiding during the day and coming out at night to hunt. If you're searching for salamanders, you might find one in the woods in a damp, rotting log, under a rock, or hiding in plants along the edge of a pond. Salamanders feed on insects, worms, and snails, which they catch with their sharp teeth. They also eat their own skin after they shed it.

There are many salamanders in North America, Europe, and Asia, a few in South America and Africa, but none at all in Australia.

Salamanders are cold-blooded, as are all of the amphibians, reptiles, and fish; their body temperature matches that of their surroundings. Although they like warm climates, they hide most of the day to avoid the hot sun. When winter comes, salamanders that live in cold climates find a safe place, such as a cave or a hollow log, crawl into it, and sleep until spring comes. Then they awake for a new mating season, ready to start new families.

Well...my salamander looks like a lizard. So, why isn't it a lizard?

Let me see... for one thing, lizards have scales, salamanders don't...

and, for another, salamanders have smooth, moist skin, lizards don't...

and, oh, yes... lizards have claws, salamanders don't.

Salamanders go through these changes while growing.

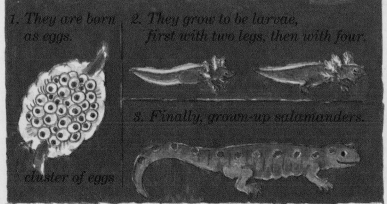

1. They are born as eggs.
2. They grow to be larvae, first with two legs, then with four.
3. Finally, grown-up salamanders.

cluster of eggs

JAPANESE GIANT SALAMANDERS, 5 ft. long, are the world's biggest. They're one of the endangered species.

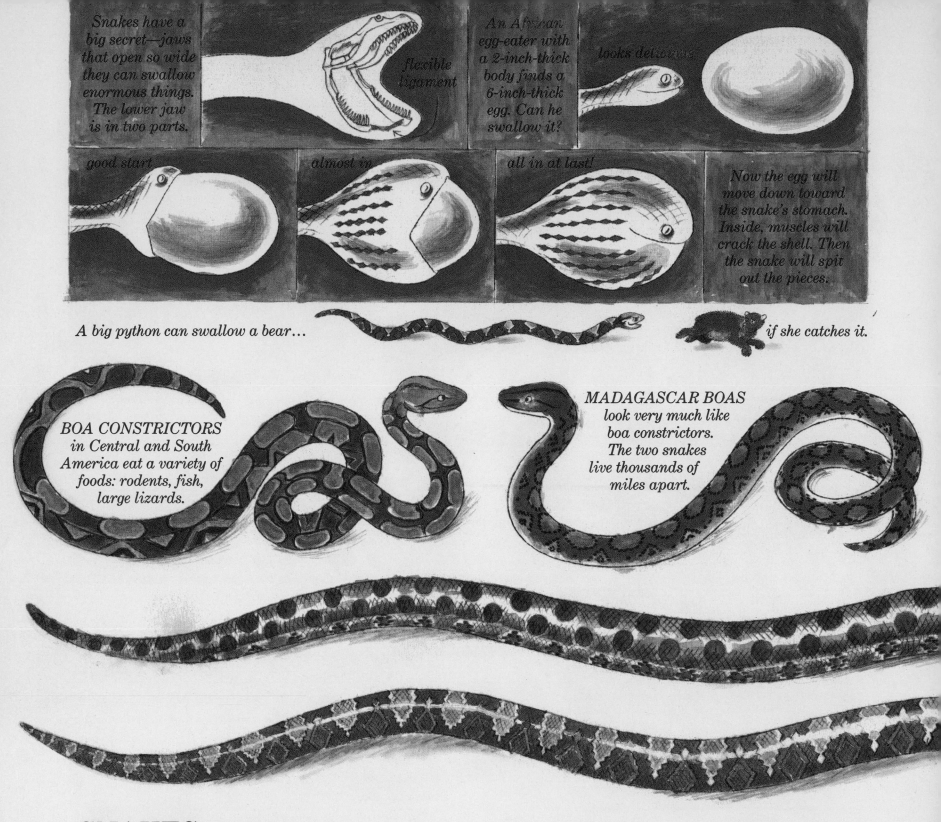

Snakes have a big secret—jaws that open so wide they can swallow enormous things. The lower jaw is in two parts.

flexible ligament

An African egg-eater with a 2-inch-thick body finds a 6-inch-thick egg. Can he swallow it?

looks delicious

good start

almost in

all in at last!

Now the egg will move down toward the snake's stomach. Inside, muscles will crack the shell. Then the snake will spit out the pieces.

A big python can swallow a bear...   if she catches it.

BOA CONSTRICTORS in Central and South America eat a variety of foods: rodents, fish, large lizards.

MADAGASCAR BOAS look very much like boa constrictors. The two snakes live thousands of miles apart.

SNAKES are reptiles. Like all reptiles, snakes are cold-blooded vertebrates. Reptiles were the first vertebrates that could survive entirely on land. Snakes and a few snake-like lizards are reptiles without legs, while turtles, most lizards, crocodiles, and alligators are reptiles with legs.

Some people think that snakes are slimy. That isn't true. Snakes are covered with a scaly skin that feels dry and smooth to the touch.

Snakes have an unusual bone structure, just suited to their curving way of crawling. Instead of the mere 26 vertebrae we have in our spine, snakes have up to 400 in theirs, and each one has 2 ribs attached to it. All these bones allow the spine to bend very gracefully as a snake crawls.

Although they can't hear most sounds coming through the air, as we can, snakes feel the vibrations in the ground caused by sounds.

As snakes grow, they shed their skins once a year and often more.

COACHWHIP SNAKES are named for their shape, long and slim like a whip. They are one of the speediest of all snakes.

EMERALD TREE BOAS catch birds up in the trees. Their green color camouflages them.

HOG-NOSED SNAKES prefer to eat toads. When threatened they roll over and pretend to be dead.

ELEPHANT'S TRUNK snakes live in the waters of Asia. They feed on fish and grow fat. On land they're almost helpless.

GRAY RAT SNAKES are harmless, but useful to people because they have a huge appetite for rats and mice.

ANACONDAS, the giant snakes of South America, are not quite the longest snakes of all, but make up for it in thickness.

RETICULATED PYTHONS in southeast Asia are the world's longest snakes, up to 33 feet.

Since they are cold-blooded, most snakes prefer the comfort of warm surroundings. In moderate climates, when winter comes, snakes hibernate in holes in the ground or in rock crevices. Sometimes hundreds of snakes hibernate in the same place.

Besides people, who often kill snakes that are actually helpful to them, snakes have many other enemies. Among them are large birds, such as eagles, and also dogs, pigs, and some other snakes.

GARTER SNAKES are easy to keep as pets. They eat earthworms.

A corn snake, with a bright new skin, leaving the old one.

Poison glands are here.

The forked tongue isn't poisonous.

Poisonous snakes have fangs: large teeth like hypodermic needles, through which they inject poison.

Avoid poisonous snakes.... They might be hiding...

behind a log,

in a hole or rock crevice,

on a ledge.

For a poisonous snakebite:

1. Get the victim to lie down.

2. Tie string above bite. 3. Apply ice. 4. Get medical help.

Black-nosed ones are poisonous.

CORAL snakes are very poisonous. This Western coral lives in the southwest U.S.

SCARLET KING snakes look very much like coral snakes but they are not poisonous.

BANDED KRAITS live in Asia. They bite only at night, and almost always bite animals, not people.

DIAMONDBACK and other **RATTLERS** shake the rattle at the end of their tails to warn anyone getting too close.

BLACK MAMBAS, the largest poisonous snakes in Africa, move through the trees with lightning speed.

POISONOUS SNAKES use their

poison to stun or kill animals for food. They have a limited supply of poison, so they don't waste it by biting people. Snakes never hunt humans—they only bite people if they feel threatened or think they are cornered. People get snakebites accidentally, as a result of carelessness or lack of knowledge. Anyone who goes to a place where there are poisonous snakes should find out all there is to know about how to avoid them. The most dangerous area in the world for fatal

snakebite is southeast Asia. In North America a fatal bite is very rare, because those people who are bitten get prompt treatment; many more people die of stings from bees and wasps.

Of the thousands of different kinds of snakes, only about 300 are poisonous. And some are more poisonous than others. The bite of a king cobra, for example, is powerful enough to kill an elephant.

Most poisonous snakes have 2 very long hollow teeth, called fangs, in their upper jaws. Inside the

TAIPANS are one of the world's biggest poisonous snakes and the most poisonous in Australia. Their favorite food is rats.

COTTONMOUTHS, also called water moccasins, live in swamps and eat fish and frogs. Their babies are not born as eggs, but as little, wriggling, fully formed snakes.

RUSSELL'S VIPERS live in the sunny parts of Asia. They hiss loudly and their fangs are even longer than the cobra's.

COPPERHEAD snakes live in the east U.S. Their main foods are mice and frogs. Their poisonous bite is serious, but people rarely die from it.

COBRAS vary in size from 3 ft. to 18 ft. Some of them can do a swaying dance to music played by a snake charmer, but, being deaf, they can't hear the music. They sway to follow the flute's movements.

snake's cheeks there are 2 small glands where the poison is made. Tubes connect these glands to the fangs. When the snake bites, the poison is squeezed out of the glands and rushes through the tubes and hollow fangs right into the wounded animal.

Snake poison, also called venom, is made into snakebite serum. The serum is used to treat people who have been bitten by poisonous snakes. Other products for medical research and treatment of diseases are made out of venom.

23

*The gecko's secret…
the bottoms of its feet
act like suction cups.*

LIZARDS are reptiles that are close relations of snakes. Like snakes, some lizards don't have legs. Others look like snakes but have legs. Many of them look like crocodiles. Even though they may look frightening, most lizards are harmless.

Lizards come in many sizes. The smallest is the tiny 2-inch-long ashy gecko. The biggest is the fierce Komodo dragon, which is 10 feet long. Lizards, like snakes, are never full-grown. They keep growing all their lives and shedding their old skin when it gets too tight.

Most lizards are insect eaters. A catch of bugs, beetles, and flies makes a good meal, but very large lizards will hunt down big animals like deer. There are also a few vegetarian lizards.

Most lizards walk with their legs spread far apart but can run very fast when they need to. Many lizards are good climbers and swimmers and some

It would be fun if there were glasses to give you chameleon vision. You could pitch to the batter while watching people on base.

dive into water from high, overhanging tree branches.

Lizards' colors usually are related to where they live. In the desert they are brown or gray and look like sand. Some lizards can change their colors quickly to blend in with their surroundings when they want to hide. Sitting very still is another thing lizards do to keep anyone from noticing them. And they have a very unusual kind of tail to help protect them. If someone grabs a lizard by the tail or steps on its tail, the tail breaks off and the lizard often escapes. In time a new tail grows.

Lizards, like all reptiles, are cold-blooded and prefer a warm climate to keep a warm body temperature. But they can't stand extreme heat and find ways to hide from the desert sun. Those that live in cooler climates have to hibernate in the winter months.

FLYING DRAGONS
can glide for 50 ft. from one tree to another. Their wings are scaly skin stretched over ribs.

FRILLED LIZARDS
spread their huge collars when they are angry or scared to make themselves look bigger and more frightening.

KOMODO DRAGONS,
10 ft. long, weighing 300 lbs., are the world's largest living lizards. They hunt and eat boar and wild pigs.

COMMON IGUANAS live in tropical America, often in trees that hang over water. When threatened, they drop into the water and swim away.

BEARDED DRAGONS' "beards" are made up of a large fold of skin with sharp spines sticking out of it.

CHAMELEONS catch insects with their long, sticky tongues.

Chameleons can change color. Each of their eyes sees separately. One eye can look ahead and the other behind at the same time.

MARINE IGUANAS are the only lizards that really live in the water. They eat seaweed and other plant life in the sea. They swim by moving their bodies like snakes, their legs held still.

BASILISKS can do the impossible—run on water. They run on their hind legs. Their feet are long and their steps are quick and light.

25

Most CROCODILES have long, thin snouts.

CROCODILES' upper and lower teeth show on the outside when their mouths are closed.

CROCODILES, ALLIGATORS,

gavials, and caimans are reptiles. All of them are also known as crocodilians. They, along with a few extra-long snakes, are the giants of the reptile world. All crocodilians look much alike. All of them can stay underwater for several hours at a time.

African crocodiles, called Nile crocodiles, are the best known. Not long ago they grew to be 33 feet long. Today so many have been killed by hunters that the biggest ones are gone and it's hard to find one over 20 feet long. Other large crocodiles are the 23-foot saltwater crocodile, which sometimes travels

hundreds of miles out into the Pacific Ocean, and the 23-foot American crocodile, which lives in Florida, Central America, and South America.

Alligators live only in the southeast United States and in China along the Yangtze River. The American alligator can be 19 feet long, but most of them are shorter. The rare Chinese alligator is about 6 feet long. In the summer, all female alligators build a big nest of leaves and mud, then lay 20 to 70 eggs in it. They guard the eggs, then care for the babies. Newly hatched babies are about 9 inches long.

Gavials are crocodilians with very long, thin

ALLIGATORS and other crocodilians swim by swinging their powerful, long tails from side to side.

On land, CROCODILIANS lie in the sun or crawl on their bellies, but can also raise their bodies and walk or run.

snouts that look like baseball bat handles. Gavials live in India, Burma, and Borneo and can grow up to 23 feet long.

Caimans come in many sizes. Dwarf caimans are under 4 feet long. Black caimans can be up to 15 feet long. Some live in slow-moving waters and mud, while others prefer rocks and rushing waters. Some of them live in shaded swamps, and others swim in sunny streams.

Crocodilians burrow into the mud of riverbanks and go into a deep sleep when the weather is too hot or too cold for their comfort.

GAVIALS have extremely long, very thin snouts, and all their teeth show when their mouths are closed.

CAIMANS are part of the alligator family. They live in Mexico, Central and South America.

ALLIGATORS have short, wide snouts.

ALLIGATORS' upper teeth show on the outside when their mouths are closed.

FRESHWATER TURTLES, *which live mostly in ponds, streams, and rivers, are smaller than sea turtles. They have legs and feet instead of flippers.*

BIG-HEADED TURTLES *have heads too big to pull into their shells.*

FLORIDA SOFT-SHELL TURTLES, *like most softshells, breathe through long, flexible noses.*

MUD TURTLES *live in southeast U.S. They are about 4 inches long.*

ALLIGATOR SNAPPING TURTLES *stay on the bottom and lure fish by wiggling their worm-like tongues.*

CHICKEN TURTLES *dart their heads out like chickens to catch food.*

RED-EARED TURTLES *come from a family with pretty shells.*

SEA TURTLES *are all big and extremely fast swimmers. They have flippers instead of feet, so move awkwardly on land, where the female goes to lay her eggs.*

LOGGERHEAD TURTLES *eat fish, snails, oysters, clams, lobsters, and crabs.*

GREEN TURTLES, *popular as human food, are now in danger of becoming extinct.*

RIDLEY TURTLES *like warm seas. Females come ashore to lay eggs on beaches of Mexico and the Guianas.*

LEATHERBACK TURTLES, *biggest of all turtles (some over 8 ft. long, weighing 2½ tons), are named for their leathery shell.*

LAND TURTLES *are called* TORTOISES. *They have a high, arched shell, and most move slowly on stubby legs. When they hibernate, they dig into the earth.*

PANCAKE TORTOISES *have flat shells, different from all other tortoise shells. They live in African mountains—great climbers!*

WEST AFRICAN TORTOISES *have a hinged back they pull down for protection.*

hinge

YELLOW-LEGGED TORTOISES *love the wet South American jungles.*

GOPHER TORTOISES *live in southern U.S. and Mexico, stay cool in tunnels they dig.*

RADIATED TORTOISES *are now very rare. They live in Madagascar.*

LEOPARD TORTOISES *live in Africa, can go far to get food. They aren't fussy and eat grass and old bones.*

PAINTED TURTLES,
brightly colored,
are popular
for tanks.

SPOTTED
TURTLES live
in quiet, fresh water
in northeast U.S.

ANNANDALE'S TURTLES are
kept in pools by people in Thailand
who have a religious belief in them.

HAWKSBILL TURTLES'
upper shell is all covered with
horny plates like shingles. This is where
we get tortoise-shell, used for combs, etc.

SEYCHELLE TORTOISES,
live on islands near Africa,
are even
bigger
than the
Galapagos
tortoises,
have a 4 ft. shell.

Tortoises don't always do well in races.

An alarmed turtle...protects itself...inside its shell.

Most turtles pull in head, legs, and tail for entire safety.

TURTLES are reptiles. Some turtles live in fresh water. Some live in salty sea water. Others, also called tortoises, live on land.

There have been turtles on earth for 150 million years—they were here before the dinosaurs. The dinosaurs disappeared many millions of years ago, but turtles are still around today, practically unchanged. They must be doing something right!

The turtle's shell, as protective as a suit of armor, may be the main reason for its survival. It is a strong, bony shell covered by a layer of horny material. The shell has 2 parts: the domed top, called the carapace, and the part underneath, called the plastron. The bones of the shoulders, spine, and ribs are fastened under the carapace. There are openings where the head, legs, and tail stick out. But these can all be pulled back into the shell very quickly if there's any threat of danger. Sea turtles, which have flippers instead of legs, can't withdraw into their shells.

Freshwater and sea turtles are good swimmers, but turtles are famous for being slow movers on land. Yet the speedy North American soft-shell turtles can run faster than people.

Turtles don't have teeth, but they do have sharp, strong beaks for tearing food apart. Their eyelids are movable; when turtles sleep the eyelids are closed. Although turtles have ear openings which are covered with a membrane, people who know a lot about them believe they are almost deaf. But they see and smell pretty well.

Turtles live a long time, especially the giant tortoises. The record is 158 years. Imagine having such a pet—you could own it, then your child could own it, then your grandchild could own it, and so on for 6 generations in all!

A mud turtle is small
enough to hold
in your hand.

A Galapagos tortoise
is big enough
to ride on.

CRABS come in many different sizes. The biggest has a leg span of 12 feet from leg to opposite leg, the smallest only ¼ inch.

Children don't really go below as deep-sea divers, but wouldn't it be fun to see these animals where they actually live?

OCTOPUSES have eyes on top of their bodies, a mouth underneath, and long arms. What looks like a face is a bag-like belly holding the heart and other organs.

COMMON SQUIDS are up to 20 inches long with 8 short arms and 2 very long ones. Like the octopuses, squids have a beaked mouth in the center of the arms.

GIANT SQUIDS can be enormous. The most gigantic one caught so far was 72 feet long. They are often attacked by sperm whales but are big enough to sometimes win.

OCTOPUSES, SQUIDS, lobsters,
crabs, shrimps, starfish, jellyfish, crayfish, cuttlefish, and horseshoe crabs are just some of the invertebrates, or animals without backbones. There are many, many more. In fact, there are 20 times as many invertebrates as there are vertebrates.

Octopuses move by forcing water out through a tube, which creates speedy jet propulsion.

Squids can squirt out dark liquid when escaping from an enemy. The liquid confuses the enemy.

Cuttlefish are related to squids and octopuses. They live in the sea close to the shore.

Jellyfish have umbrella-shaped bodies and long, stinging tentacles which hang down and trap food.

Starfish don't all have 5 arms; some have as few as 4 and others have as many as 50.

Lobsters, shrimps, crayfish, and crabs, which all have jointed shells, are called crustaceans. All of

American lobster

Norway lobster

SHRIMPS *are much like lobsters and crayfish, but smaller and without their big claws.*

LOBSTERS *have 2 large claws. One is used for crushing, the other for picking and scraping.*

STARFISH *have a star-shaped mouth in the center of their underside.*

GIANT JELLYFISH, *whose tentacles are up to 200 feet long, are among the largest sea animals. They live in icy arctic waters and have a dangerous sting.*

In spite of their names, jellyfish, starfish, cuttlefish, and crayfish are not fish at all.

CUTTLEFISH *develop stripes in the mating season or to hide in seaweed.*

CRAYFISH *live mostly in fresh water, but there are some saltwater kinds.*

HORSESHOE CRABS *are not crabs. They are prehistoric animals that haven't changed for millions of years. Their nearest cousins are spiders.*

them have 10 legs, 4 feelers, and eyes on stalks.

Crabs live mainly in the ocean. However, there are some freshwater crabs and just a few land crabs.

Horseshoe crabs walk along the bottom of shallow ocean waters. They can also swim upside-down.

Shrimps also are mostly ocean inhabitants. They swim backward, waving their fan tails.

Crayfish look like small lobsters. Unlike lobsters, however, crayfish live in fresh water.

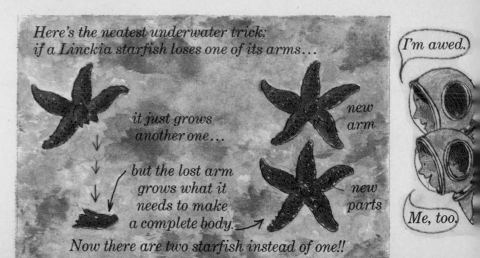

Here's the neatest underwater trick: if a Linckia starfish loses one of its arms...

it just grows another one...

but the lost arm grows what it needs to make a complete body.

new arm

new parts

Now there are two starfish instead of one!!

I'm awed.

Me, too.

Big clam shells make good digging tools.

What kind is it?

Shell collecting is a very enjoyable hobby.

SUPER SHELLS
START A COLLECTION

Is it really the sound of the sea?

calico scallop

ornate scallops

American oysters

black scallop

SCALLOPS can jet-propel themselves through the water to escape their enemy—the starfish. Their eyes are in rows just inside their shells.

pilgrim scallop

European oysters

Edible OYSTERS and other shellfish are an important part of many people's diet. Special pearl oysters in warm seas are the only kind that produce valuable pearls.

tubes with suction cups at the ends

great pearl oyster

cherrystone clam

CLAMS vary in size from about ½ inch up to giant clams more than 4 feet long, weighing over 400 pounds. Clams eat as scallops, oysters, and mussels do. They let in water filled with tiny plant and animal life, called plankton, through a tube. They keep what they want, then force the rest out.

quahog clam

32

Clams, oysters, and scallops are victims of the starfish that wraps them in its arms and pulls their shells apart to get at them.

pismo clam

calico clam

duck clams

Sand castles can be decorated with shells.

Oh, thank you.

Finding just the shell you're looking for often takes a lot of patience.

SCALLOPS, OYSTERS, mussels,

clams, and snails are mollusks that have hard, tough shells to protect their soft bodies. There are other mollusks, such as squids and octopuses, that don't have protective shells but have small shells inside their bodies. Scallops, oysters, mussels, and clams have both a top and a bottom shell which are held together by strong muscles. The double shell is called a bivalve. Snails have only one coiled shell, called a univalve. Some mollusks don't have shells at all. All mollusks are invertebrates.

Shellfish, both the mollusks and the crustaceans (those with jointed shells—lobsters, crabs, and others), have always been an important source of food for people in most parts of the world.

Each kind of mollusk grows its own special kind of shell and the shell keeps growing as long as the animal lives. Most shells are made of an outer, middle, and inner layer of material. Often the inner layer is smooth, shiny and full of shimmering colors. People call it "mother-of-pearl," and make buttons, jewelry, and pocketknife handles out of it.

Shell collecting is a hobby that many people enjoy. They mostly collect mollusk shells. Finding them on the beach is the most fun, but there are shops that sell the more unusual shells.

If you were a collector you might like the univalve shell of a horse conch—it's 2 feet long! Or maybe you'd prefer some tiny Barlia snail shells—50 of them, side by side, take up only 2 inches. You might pick a bivalve, like the giant South Pacific clam shell, which is 4 feet long. Or the smallest bivalve might appeal to you—it's the North American turton clam, just 1/8 of an inch long.

Most MUSSELS live in the ocean, often near rocky shores. They can attach themselves to the rocks with threads their bodies make.

blue mussels

horse mussel

moon snail

marbled cone

dogwinkle

SNAILS have just one coiled shell. They come in many shapes, colors, and sizes. A snail travels with its shell on its back, and retreats into the shell if there is any sign of danger.

tulip snail

33

whelk

PARTS OF AN ANT — *thorax* *head* *antennae* *abdomen* *jaws* *mouth* *back legs* *middle legs* *front legs*

ANTS are insects. There are more than a million known species of insects in the world. All of them have bodies that are divided into 3 parts—head, thorax, and abdomen. On the head are 2 antennae, which are used to taste, feel, and smell, 2 compound eyes that are made up of thousands of separate little eyes, and a pair of jaws that open and close sideways. Attached to the thorax are 3 pairs of legs and (usually) 2 pairs of wings. The abdomen holds the stomach and other inner organs.

Ants have lived on earth for 100 million years. They have spread to almost every part of the world and thrive in almost any environment. There are 15,000 kinds of ants, ranging in size from 1/25 of an inch to 1-1/2 inches long. Most ants are black, red, or brown. Some ants don't have wings.

Ants live in groups called colonies. A colony may have a few ants or as many as 100,000 of them.

HARVESTER ants gather seeds and carry them into the nest.

INSIDE UNDERGROUND ANT NESTS
What many kinds of ants do underground (but not all in the same nest, of course):

Harvesters store seeds for future eating.

more harvesters

Some ants take care of larvae while others tend cocoons.

Ant eggs are handled with care.

Trash is brought here.

In winter ants huddle tight and sleep until spring.

Crickets and other insects are sometimes ants' guests.

← *This is not what they look like.*
This is. →

CARPENTER ants chew up wood. They don't eat it. With their powerful jaws they carve rooms for themselves, in trees outdoors and in wooden beams indoors.

← *This is not what they look like.*
This is. →

ARMY ants march in huge groups of many thousands. Animals of all sizes, from roaches to deer, are eaten if they don't escape. People leave their homes to get out of the ants' way.

In spring, ants ready to become queens, accompanied by males, swarm out of the nest, then mate. When a queen lands, she begins to lay eggs and a new family is started.

Different kinds of ants build different kinds of nests. Some nests are underground, some above ground. Sometimes ants build a nest that is partly above ground and partly below.

A new colony is begun by an ant ready to become a queen. In the spring she flies out of her nest with many other ants. While she is flying, a male mates with her. She lands, bites off her own wings (she won't need them any more), and finds a place for a nest. She digs a hole, enters it, and closes the entrance with soil. Then she lays her eggs. Each egg hatches into a larva. The larva becomes a pupa, and from the pupa comes an adult. In this group of adults there are queens, males, and workers. The queens are larger than the others, and eventually will start a new nest. The males do no work; their only job is to mate with a queen. The workers, all females, lay no eggs, but do all the work in and out of the nest.

LEAFCUTTER ants cut out pieces of leaves and carry them into the nest.

The queen is cleaned, fed, and fondled by her attendants.

Leafcutters chew up and pile their leaves.

Mushrooms grow in chewed-up leaves.

storing honey

HONEY ants bring honey to the nest. They store some in ants who hang from the ceiling. Hanging ants become honey barrels, ready to feed others.

Aphids, protected by ants, supply them with food.

Trash is brought here.

more honey ants

This is not what they look like.
This is. ⟶

FARMER ants, called leafcutters, bring pieces of leaves into their nests. They chew the leaves, pile them up, and from the piles grow mushrooms—their food.

TO STUDY ANTS you have to be able to see what goes on inside an ant nest. Two pieces of glass with some earth framed between them make a practical, visible nest after you add the ants.

35

BEES are insects that live almost everywhere except near the freezing North and South Poles. Although there are 10,000 kinds of bees, only honeybees make honey — a very tasty food, ask any bear.

Bees have 5 eyes — a big compound eye on either side of their head and 3 little ones on top. A bee's tongue is like a tube and is used for sucking nectar up from flowers. The bee's poison-carrying stinger sticks out of its abdomen. Only females have stingers, which they use in self-defense.

In a colony of honeybees there is a single queen and many workers and drones. The queen is the mother of the colony. All the other bees are her children. The workers, which are all female, make beeswax and build the honeycomb nest, do the housework, tend young bees, and feed all the bees in the colony. They gather nectar from flowers to make honey, and also gather pollen. They guard the nest from enemies. The drones, which are all male, do nothing but eat, rest, and wait for the summer mating season. Then they fly away from the nest to mate with a young queen.

A bee grows fast. The queen lays a tiny egg. Soon it's a larva. Workers feed it until it becomes a pupa.

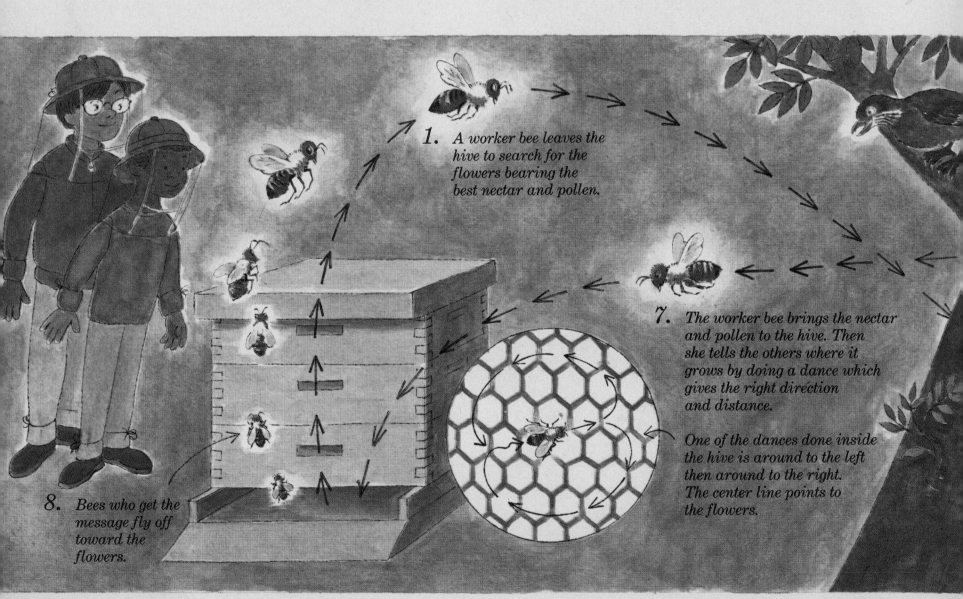

1. *A worker bee leaves the hive to search for the flowers bearing the best nectar and pollen.*

7. *The worker bee brings the nectar and pollen to the hive. Then she tells the others where it grows by doing a dance which gives the right direction and distance.*

One of the dances done inside the hive is around to the left then around to the right. The center line points to the flowers.

8. *Bees who get the message fly off toward the flowers.*

The ENEMIES of BEES attack them or steal honey. Robber flies, dragonflies, praying mantises, and kingbirds can catch bees in mid-air. Mice break into the hive for honey. Toads catch bees with their flip-out tongues. Skunks lure bees out of the hive. Bears can destroy the hive to get honey.

dragonflies

robber flies

Finally it's an adult. It takes 21 days for an adult worker to develop and 24 days for an adult drone to form. The queen takes only 16 days to develop.

Sometimes a bee colony becomes too crowded. The queen decides to leave and build a new nest. Many of the workers swarm out of the colony with the queen, leaving other workers behind to select new queens from among the larvae. One of these will become the new queen of the colony.

Some kinds of bees don't live in big colonies. There are no workers. The female builds her own nest and tends her own eggs.

The only QUEEN in the beehive lays every one of the eggs.

The WORKER bees, many thousands of females, do all work.

DRONES, all males, do no work but mate with the new queen.

Bees, on their own, nest in a tree, cave, or other shelter.

Long ago beekeepers began to supply bees with basketry hives.

Now they use wood box hives. Honey is removed more easily.

4. *Ah! She sees just the kind of flowers she was looking for.*

5. *The worker bee lands on the flowers, sucks up all the nectar she can carry, and loads pollen on her hind legs.*

6. *Now she's flying straight for home.*

3. *More searching*

2. *Still searching*

frogs and toads

skunks

kingbirds

praying mantises

mice

bears

spring azure

purple emperor

blue morpho

1. Butterflies fly in the DAYTIME.

question mark

2. Butterfly ANTENNAE are thin with bumps at the ends.

swallowtail

buckeye

painted lady

3. Butterfly BODIES are thin.

fritillary

red-spotted purple

4. Butterfly WINGS are held upright at rest.

orange sulphur

monarch

Butterfly CATERPILLARS are as varied as butterflies are.

swallowtail   zebra   monarch   buckeye   sulphur   pipevine

BUTTERFLIES are insects that live

in all parts of the world. There are 90,000 kinds of butterflies, with wingspreads from 12 inches to less than 1/2 inch. Tiny scales on its wings make up each butterfly's pattern of colors.

Many flowers need pollen from other blossoms to produce new seeds and flowers. Butterflies fly from flower to flower, feeding on nectar and spreading pollen that sticks to their bodies. In their hungry caterpillar stage, some kinds of butterflies eat crops.

A butterfly has a handy device like a curled-up straw which it can uncurl from its mouth to sip nectar from flowers. A butterfly cannot bite or chew. Nectar and other liquids are its only food.

In winter some butterflies migrate to warm climates, traveling in large flocks and often flying long distances. Others find a sheltered place where they can hibernate for the winter.

Moths and butterflies are born as eggs laid in clusters or singly.

Eating steadily, they become full-grown caterpillars.

1. Moths fly at NIGHT.

2. Moth ANTENNAE are <u>feathery</u>.

3. Moth BODIES are <u>thick</u>.

4. Moth WINGS are held <u>flat</u> at rest.

magpie

napata

clothes moth

erasmia

acrea

polyphemus

silkworm moth

imperial

luna

Cynthia

garden tiger

gypsy

underwing

Moth CATERPILLARS are as varied as moths are.

moon silk

urota

cinnabar

buck

luna

Isabella (woolly bear)

MOTHS are also insects that live almost everywhere. There are about 10,000 different kinds of moths. They are about the same size as butterflies, but one kind of moth is tinier than any butterfly — its wingspread is only 1/10 of an inch.

Caterpillars of both moths and butterflies spin silken threads through a spinneret that sticks out below their mouths. Silkworm moth caterpillars spin threads that people make into fine silk fabrics.

Moth caterpillars form a cocoon, butterflies a chrysalis.

Moths pollinate flowers just as butterflies do. But moths can also be destructive. Moth caterpillars named tent caterpillars make their nests in trees, then eat all the leaves. Moth caterpillars called cutworms destroy cotton, corn, and fruit crops. Clothes moth caterpillars prefer to eat your best woolen sweater or rugs and furs in the house. When moth caterpillars grow into adult moths, they no longer do any harm.

A total change: out come butterflies or moths.

Only the female mosquito bites and buzzes.

MOSQUITOES are flying insects.

There are about 1,500 kinds of mosquitoes. They live everywhere on earth, except in very cold places.

Female mosquitoes are larger than males. It is the female that bites people and animals, and if she is carrying a disease, she may pass it along. She bites and sucks some blood out to help produce her eggs. When she bites, she pumps her saliva into the blood of her victim to make the blood easier to suck up. Saliva is the thing that makes the bite itch.

Mosquito eggs are laid on water. Soon the eggs become wriggling larvae. The larvae grow for 3 weeks and then turn into pupae. The pupae float for a week until adults develop and fly off. The adults mate soon after. They have to — the male lives only 2 weeks. Females live for 3 to 5 months.

Fleas are terrific jumpers.

a dog flea enlarged 25 times

FLEAS are very small insects.

They are less than 1/8 of an inch long. Fleas cannot fly, as they have no wings, but they make up for it by their great jumping power. They can jump 13 inches — that's more than 100 times their size. Guess how far you would jump if you could leap like a flea. Multiply your height by 100 to get close to the answer.

Fleas live on dogs, cats, rats, chickens, birds, horses, many other animals, and people. Most fleas can jump from one animal to another. Fleas eat blood that they suck out of the animal they live on. By feeding on infected animals and then finding a new home on people, fleas can spread diseases from one to the other. Keeping your pets clean by bathing them with insecticide soap will help to keep them free of annoying fleas.

stable fly—bites animals and us

housefly—bites no one

FLIES are insects with wings. There are 85,000 kinds of flies.

Houseflies are tan and black and grow to be about 1/4 inch long. The female housefly lays her eggs, 100 of them at a time, in animal dung, garbage, or other waste. It takes about 2 weeks for the eggs to develop into adults — so houseflies multiply very fast. Because they grow up in unsanitary conditions, then crawl on food, houseflies can spread disease.

Stable flies look very much like houseflies. But if you think you were bitten by a housefly, you're wrong — it had to be a stable fly, because houseflies don't bite. Most stable flies grow up in barns. Their eggs are laid and develop in animal dung. Stable flies spread diseases to people. Their bite is very painful to cows, horses, and humans.

Roaches were here on earth before people.

ROACHES look exactly the same today as they did millions of years ago. They are part of a large insect family found all over the world. Roaches are brown or black and measure from 1/2 inch to 2 inches long. Although most roaches have wings that lie flat against their body, most of them don't fly.

In warm climates, some roaches live outdoors, making their homes in the moist earth. Indoor varieties are household pests that spoil food and have an unpleasant odor. They hide all day in damp, warm places, usually near pipes, and come out at night to eat. Their food is garbage, paper, bookbindings, clothing, and whatever humans eat. To get rid of roaches, be neat with food and garbage, seal spaces around pipes, check grocery bags and laundry bundles, spray roaches' hideouts with insecticide.

BEETLES are the most varied group of insects. There are 290,000 different kinds. They live all over the world — on land, in water, and underground. Most beetles have a hard shell, which is a sort of insect suit of armor and protects them from attack. Beetles look as if they have no wings because wing coverings that look like a shell hide their folded-up wings. The wing coverings usually have bold patterns and bright or metallic colors that match the rest of the body. When the beetle is flying, the hard coverings are held out of the way and the wings underneath unfold and straighten out.

Beetles vary in size, which is from 1/50 of an inch to 6-1/2 inches long. A beetle's mouth is equipped to bite and chew. Most beetles stick to a vegetarian diet, eating plants only. Others eat worms and insects, and the bodies of small animals serve as food for their larvae.

Some vegetarian beetles are very destructive. The boll weevils, for example, can be extremely harmful to cotton crops. Both adult boll weevils and their larvae (called grubs) consume large quantities of cotton plants. Grubs of carpet beetles devour carpets. But many kinds of beetles eat insects that destroy plants and crops. The ladybird, also called ladybug, is one of these garden helpers.

Fireflies, which are also called lightning bugs, are beetles which can give off light.

Fireflies, also called lightning bugs, are really beetles.

Chemical actions in the abdomen make these beetles light up. Glowworms are wingless female fireflies.

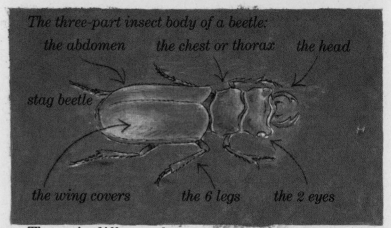

The three-part insect body of a beetle:
the abdomen   the chest or thorax   the head
stag beetle
the wing covers   the 6 legs   the 2 eyes

The main difference between beetles and other insects is that beetles have wing coverings over their wings.

HOW A BEETLE GETS READY, THEN STARTS FLYING

Beetles look as if they cannot fly because their wings are hidden. But they do fly, though slowly and not too gracefully.

4. and away it flies.

3. Wings unfold and stretch...

tiger beetle

2. Wing covers lift and reveal folded wings.

1. A beetle, planning to fly, goes through several steps.

just a few of the more than 290,000 kinds of beetles

ladybug   unicorn beetle   snout beetle   potato beetle   may beetle   sexton beetle

SPIDERS look like insects, but belong to a different class of animals called arachnids.

Not all spiders make webs, but all spiders are able to spin silken threads. One kind of spider spins a line of silk with a ball of sticky stuff at the end. An insect flies by, and the spider swings the line at it. The ball sticks to the insect and the spider hauls it in. Some young spiders travel by spinning long silk lines which the wind catches. The young spiders, still attached, sail off into the air for a sort of balloon ride.

Although spiders kill insects by biting them and injecting poison, only a very few spiders have poisons strong enough to harm people. The black widow spider is one of them. Most spiders are useful to people because they destroy mosquitoes, flies, and other insects that carry dangerous diseases.

Each kind of spider builds a different kind of silk-lined nest as its home. The trapdoor spider builds underground tunnels lined with silk and spins a door equipped with hinges and handles on the inside so it can pull the door shut.

There are more than 30,000 kinds of spiders. They range in size from those almost too small to see, to those measuring 10 inches from outer leg to outer leg. They live almost everywhere: on mountains, in water, wherever they find food. Most live for a year, dying in winter. As pets, however, some spiders have lived for 20 years.

Entomologists are scientists who specialize in insects. Arachnidologists are scientists who specialize in spiders.

Spiders have no antennae, the feelers that insects have. Instead, they feel with the straight hairs on their legs.

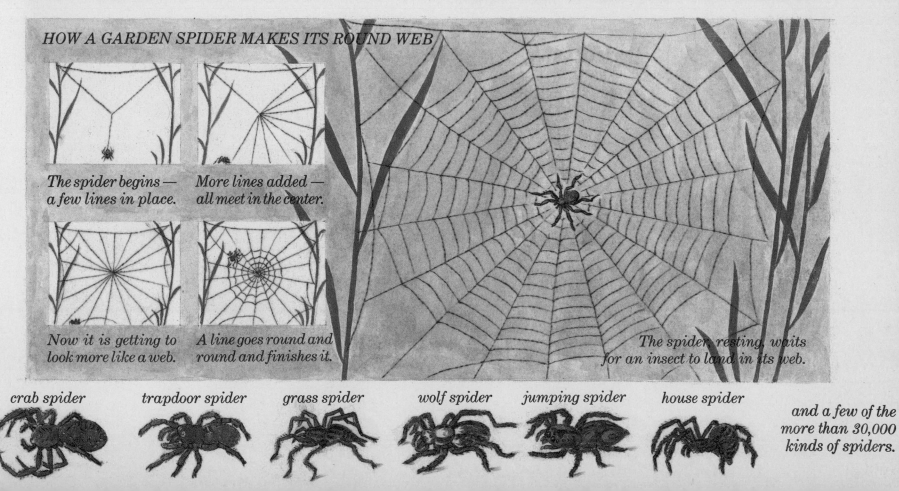

HOW A GARDEN SPIDER MAKES ITS ROUND WEB

The spider begins — a few lines in place.

More lines added — all meet in the center.

Now it is getting to look more like a web.

A line goes round and round and finishes it.

The spider, resting, waits for an insect to land in its web.

crab spider

trapdoor spider

grass spider

wolf spider

jumping spider

house spider

and a few of the more than 30,000 kinds of spiders.

The FUTURE for the animal kingdom might be very dismal and depressing. If people stopped trying to improve our environment, the air, water, and land would become even more polluted than they are now. Nature's wonderful system of life — with all living things working in harmony — would break down. Healthy plants couldn't grow in polluted soil; plant-eating animals couldn't thrive on a diet of unhealthy plants; meat-eating animals would sicken on a bad food supply. Insects, fish, mammals, birds, and other animals would become fewer and fewer. One by one, they would die out and people would have the earth to themselves, with enough food stored to last a long time. But there would be no pets, no zoos, no animals on land, in the sea, or in the air — and people would be pretty sad!

THE LION COMPLETELY VANISHED, TOO BAD

The CROCODILES have all died out, never to be seen again

THE PENGUIN VERY EXTINCT

THE MUD SNAKE AND ALL OTHER SNAKES NOW DEFUNCT

THE MARINE IGUANA Gone forever but not forgotten

OR, life in the future could be peaceful and happy if enough people join the growing movement to save what is good in our environment and restore what has been spoiled. Run-down forests can be replanted, polluted waters and air made pure again. We can save, then help preserve, animals that are becoming rare.

Work on this problem, begun many years ago, is going on today. In 1900, there were 40,000 Bengal tigers. Not long ago there were only 2,000 of them, but hard work turned the tide and their numbers are increasing. In 1940, only 15 whooping cranes were alive, but now there are 10 times as many. Although lions and lambs may never be best friends, with our help the animal kingdom can survive and people and animals can enjoy a peaceful, happy future together.

You are looking for some new specimens
for your butterfly collection.
How can you tell butterflies from moths?
(See pages 38-39)

You are kissing a frog,
hoping that it will turn into a prince.
But are you sure it isn't a toad?
Can you tell one from the other?
(See page 16)

You are doing a little underwater exploring.
Suddenly you are face to face with the biggest of all fish.
Should you be worried?
(See page 14)